get creative

Start Beading & Jewellery Making

Contents

Peyote Triangle Bracelet
Page 73

Bicone Triangle Bracelet
Page 106

Welcome

get creative

Cleopatra Necklace
Page 44

Grace Crystal Necklace
Page 62

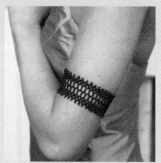

Hexagonal Arm Band
Page 66

Projects to Make

Waves Necklace • Page 9

Welcome

The Get Creative series of books is designed to inspire and assist you in making fantastic craft and DIY projects at home, either on your own or with friends and family. Making things yourself allows you to bring your own flare and personal tastes to a project and, with our new Start Beading and Jewellery Making book, you can also save hundreds of dollars along the way.

Beading is something that appeals to a number of age groups and is a perfect pastime for youngsters, teenagers and adults and can be done in groups or solo. This book allows you to create your own looks, at a fraction of the cost, and coordinate to match your wardrobe.

Our Get Creative team has had a ball working on Start Beading and Jewellery Making and we hope you can see this in the results. By learning the basic principles of beading and jewellery construction you can master the projects within this book but also go on to create truly unique works of fashion and art for you and your loved ones.

Whether you're after a very simple 'petal necklace', a 'Cleopatra' look or even an 'amulet bag', you'll find something to appeal inside Start Beading and Jewellery Making.

We've included a little background information on where various beads come from and what their best uses are as well as a comprehensive guide to the foundations of beading such as 'flat netting', 'Peyote stitching' and 'right angle weaving' so you can sound like an expert and, more importantly, go on to create your own designs down the track.

So, lets get creative and enjoy!
Jono, Veronica and the Get Creative team

P.S. To help you we have included the table below converting grams to ounces and centimetres to inches. We have also included a diagram legend on page 127 to show you what all symbols stand for.

Converting Grams to Ounces	Converting Centimetres to Inches
30g = approx. 1 ounce	2.5cm = 1"
Multiply grams value by 0.035 to get ounces	Multiply cm value by 0.03937 to get inches

Beads

Beads come in a large variety of sizes, shapes and finishes.

Size 11 Seed Bead

Size 8 Seed Bead

Seed Beads are round donut-shaped beads that range in size. These are often perfect for strung necklaces. You can use them as spacers on each side of a large bead to make it stand out or string them in a group as part of a necklace's design.

Seed beads have been manufactured in many sizes. The largest size is 5° (also known as E beads), which are about 5mm wide to the smallest size, which is 20° or 22°, which are not much larger than a grain of sand. The larger the number of the bead, the smaller the size of the bead is. Beads smaller than 15° have not been made for about 100 years. The most commonly available size in the widest range of colours is 11°. (The symbol o stands for naught or zero. The greater the number of naughts, for example 22°, the smaller the bead.)

Seed beads can have a matte or shiny finish and include opaque, a solid coloured glass. Transparent beads are made of coloured glass through which light can pass. They can also be lined with coloured glass or a coloured, dyed or painted lining. Silver-lined or gold-lined seed beads are lined with real silver or gold. Transparent beads, and opaque beads, may also be treated with a variety of coatings. These include: iris or aurora borealis (AB) or lustre, which gives a multi-coloured effect; opalescent or pearlised; metallic (coloured metal is fused to the glass surface); or galvanized (a rich but impermanent metallic coating).

It is recommended that you test beads for colourfastness by washing, rubbing and putting them in sunlight, nail polish remover, or bleach.

The best round seed beads are made in Japan and the Czech Republic. Czech seed beads are usually more irregular and rounder than Japanese seed beads, which are a bit squared-off in shape. Czech beads produce a bumpier surface when woven together, but they reflect light at a wider range of angles. They can also be chosen to fill different sized spaces more easily. The rounder shape makes them ideal for right-angle weave. Japanese seed beads produce a more uniform surface and texture. Japanese and Czech seed beads can be used together, but a Japanese seed bead is slightly larger than the same-sized Czech bead.

Japanese Seed Beads come in a sparklier cut version. They are formed with six sides and are called hex-cut or hex beads. The cut on the Czech beads are less regular, and they are called 2-cuts or 3-cuts. Charlottes have an irregular facet-cut on one side of the bead.

A newer kind of seed bead was invented in the late 1980s by Mr Masayoshi Katsuoka of Miyuki Shoji Co. The generic term for this bead is Japanese cylinder bead, but other names for it are the Delica (the Miyuki brand) or Antique or Toho Antique or Magnifica (the brand name of Miyuki's competitor Toho). Japanese cylinder beads come in hundreds of colours and finishes, including plated with high-carat gold.

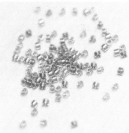

Delica Bead

Cylinder beads are extremely popular for peyote stitch projects such as amulet purses because of their great regularity and their extremely large holes. They fit together almost seamlessly, producing a smooth, fabric-like surface. The bead is normally labelled size 11°, but is really about the size of a Czech 12° - if you want to use it with round seed beads. In the mid 1990s, Toho Company began making the 3.3 cylinder bead, so named because it is 3.3mm long. Miyuki calls its similar bead a size 8° Delica. Both sizes of cylinder beads 11° and 8° are also available as hex-cuts.

Austrian Swarovski Crystals are beads made from high-quality leaded glass and cut with precise facets like precious stones.

Bugle Beads are thin tubes of glass. Size 1 bugles are about 2mm long, but you can find bugle beads that are even longer than 30mm. Bugles can be faceted or hex-cut, straight or twisted. The selection of colours, shapes, sizes and finishes is more limited than that of the seed beads.

Bugle Bead

Drop Beads can look like a teardrop, or have a moulded or pressed shape.

Bicone Beads look like two round cone shapes joined together at the wide end of the cone.

6mm Bicone Bead   4mm Bicone Bead

Lampwork Beads were named because of the smaller torch used in their manufacturing compared with furnaces. These are made individually.

Feature Beads come in a variety of shapes and sizes, from flowers, leaves, shells etc. to large decorative beads.

Pearl Beads start from 2mm to 12mm and come in a variety of shapes and colours. Freshwater pearls come in a variety of styles. Prices on pearls vary according to quality.

Feature Bead   Pearl Bead

Threads for Bead Weaving

Bead weaving threads need to be strong and thin because they endure a lot of abrasion during weaving, and the bead hole must accommodate 2 - 4 (sometimes more) passes of thread through it. The two most popular and available threads are Nymo, Size B or D, and Silamide, which is available only in size A. In Australia Silamide is difficult to find but the KayGee thread extra fine is about the equivalent. Remember, the earlier the letter in the alphabet, the thinner the thread, except size O, which is thinner than A. All types of threads are nylon. Nymo is a filament thread, which means that long fibres of nylon run side by side. Silamide is a two-strand plied (twisted) thread and comes from the tailoring industry. Both are available in many colours. KayGee is a twisted thread and is available in a small range of colours.

Nymo is easier to thread because it can be flattened. Silamide and KayGee threads remain round. All will build up twist that must be released periodically as you work. Because of their round verses flat profiles, Silamide will fill bead holes with fewer passes than Nymo B. If you want the beadwork to be stiff, this is an important consideration.

Other strong threads are used by some beaders, though they are harder to find.

Match the thread colour to the beads whenever possible. If your design has a lot of colours, choose a neutral colour like ash or tan. Usually choose a slightly darker shade of thread than the bead colour, so that the thread disappears between the beads.

Beading Needles

Just like seed beads, the higher the number, the finer the beading needle. Most beaders prefer English beading needles because they are the most flexible. Unlike sewing needles, the eye area of a beading needle is almost as narrow as its shaft. If you work mostly with cylinder beads, you can use a thicker needle than is possible when weaving Czech seed beads, which often don't accommodate the eye of a size 10 needle. As you become comfortable with seed beads, you will use size 12 or 13 needles. They are harder to thread but easier to use than a size 10. Size 15 needles are often necessary when using very small beads (Czech 14° or smaller). For bead embroidery you may prefer a short needle such as a size 12 or a sharp needle.

Twisted Wire Needles

These are made from a length of fine wire folded in half and twisted tightly together. They have a large open eye at the fold, which is easy to thread. The eye flattens when you pull the needle though the first bead.

Starting and Ending Thread

This will vary according to the technique that you are using.

For right angle weave: Start out with a long piece of thread. If you use a double needle method (for example, a needle at each end of a piece of thread), you can use twice as long a piece of thread since you will use half in each needle. Single thread the needles and pull thread down to a comfortable working length. When your thread or wire gets short, change it in the middle of a row rather than at the end. Work the threads back through the piece following the pattern and tie a small knot. Work through a little further and tie another small knot. If you're not right against a bead, you can often pull the knot into the bead so it will not show. Place a dot of glue or nail polish on the thread and pull it through the last bead or two and cut. It helps to secure the thread if you turn away from the row that you are working on. Starting a new thread in a double needle method is easy. Centre the thread on the last pattern worked and continue beading. For single needles, bury the tail of the new thread in the work and come out where you are to continue beading.

For peyote: Zigzag through beads. End in the direction that you are going and then reverse the direction a couple of times before cutting the thread. When weaving in neck straps or fringe threads, make careful knots for added security. You can leave short tails as you work and trim them later. This will allow you to see where you ended and started, and to avoid having too many thread endings and beginnings in the same area.

This handy chart explains what size needle and thread you should usually use with specific seed bead and bugle bead sizes.

	Beads getting bigger, bugles longer & needles & thread fatter ← Beads getting smaller, bugles shorter & needles & thread thinner →		
Seed beads	6, 8, 10	11,12 (delicas)	13, 14, 15
Beading needles	#10	#11, #28 tapestry	#13, 15-16
Thread	Nymo FF, F, EE, E KayGee medium/thick	Nymo D KayGee Fine	Nymo OO, OOOO KayGee Extra Fine
Bugles in mm	30, 25 ,20	12, 9, 7	6, 5,
Czech bugles	#5 (11 mm)	#3 (7 mm)	#2 (4 mm)

Don't just use the chart to figure out what size thread and needles to use with your beads The number of times a needle and thread needs to pass through the bead determines how fine a needle and thread you actually need.

Tiger Tail
Plastic coated stainless steel wire of varying thickness. Available in clear (silver) or coloured eg. red, gold, black. Used with heavier beads, and should be crimped, not knotted.

Tiger Tail

Findings

The word 'findings' is used to collectively describe a variety of items such as jump rings, bead tips and clasps. These come in silver, gold or nickel. The quality of findings can vary greatly so it is best to buy the finding most suited to the piece you are making.

Bead Tips

Also called 'ending'. Bead tips or calottes are used at the end of a strand to conceal a knot, and to connect the strand to the clasp. These bead tips are a small metal-contained bead that comes in either a basket shape, or a two sided clam shell shape. They are available in small and large sizes. The size to be used is determined by the size of the knot to be concealed.

The bead tip goes on first before the first bead. Enter the bead tip from the top down, leaving enough thread so that a knot can be easily made. Tie the thread into one or two good knots. Cut the thread close to the knot and apply a small drop of glue (or nail polish to the knot. Slide the bead tip firmly against the knot and close the shell part, making sur that the knot is fully concealed. The other tip goes on after all the beads have been strung

Bell Caps

These look just like small bells, with a loop at the top. Bell caps are used when a fringe of beads, such as a tassel, is incorporated into the design, and the cap is an attractive way to collect and conceal the ends of the fringe that is being attached.

Cones

These are usually made of metal and look like pointed ice cream cones with openings at both ends. They are ideal for concealing the end and knots of multiple strand necklaces and joining it attractively to a clasp.

Head Pins

The head pin is a length of wire with a flat or decorated head at one end to keep the bead from falling off. It is used to string a bead or several beads then connect them to a strand or finding by making a loop at the open end. They come in different diameters and lengths ranging from 2.5cm-7.6cm (1"-3").

Eye Pins

Exactly like head pins except they have a round loop on one end instead of a head. This can be used to attach other pins when forming a linked piece, or for earrings.

Eye Pins

Jump Rings

These serve as connectors whether between beads alone, or as a link between the bead tip and the clasp. The jump ring is simply a small circle of wire with a slit that allows it to be opened for connecting. They come in different sizes depending on the application.

It is essential that the jump ring be opened correctly. The jump ring should never be pulled apart in opposing directions, as this will pull the ring out of shape, making it very difficult to close properly. To open a jump ring, hold one side of the ring with pliers, and then move the other side of the ring sideways with another pair of pliers. Use a slight twisting motion. To close the ring reverse the process, ensuring that the ends meet close to each other.

Split Rings

Split Rings

These are used like jump rings, but they are much more secured. They look like tiny key rings and are made of springy wire.

Crimp Beads

These are small, large holed, thin walled, metal beads. These are designed to be able to be flattened, or rolled into a tight roll. Use these instead of knots when stringing jewellery on flexible beading wire.

Crimp Beads

Findings

Findings

Clasps

Clasps come in a wide variety of sizes and styles. Some clasps connect both ends of a single strand; some connect several strands individually, while others can accommodate a wide rope of several strands together. Generally, the clasp has one or more small loops on either side for attaching to a single strand per loop. Clasps can be simple or very ornate, all metal or covered with stones.

Some clasps are made so they are not seen as a clasp but as part of the design. Some of the most common are the toggle (consisting of a ring and a bar), the parrot clasp (or lobster claw) the bolt ring (which opens when you push on a tiny lever), the S-hook (which links two soldered rings or split rings) and the hook and eye.

Bolt Ring

Parrot Clasp

Barrel Clasp

Clasp Tags

Earrings

These come in a huge variety of metals and styles, including post, French hook, kidney wire, and hoop. You will almost always want a loop on earring findings to attach beads.

Shepherds Hook

Clip On

Connectors

Connectors allow you to have multi-strand necklaces attached to a clasp neatly.

Bead Caps

Bead caps are decorative caps for feature beads to give them a different appearance.

Connectors

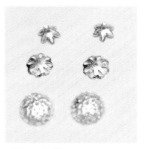

Bead Caps

Pliers

Chain-nose pliers (round on the outside and flat on the inside) can help pull a needle through a bead with a small hole, or one that has been packed tight with thread. Be careful not to pull too hard as some beads can break under pressure. They are also often used to add jewellery "findings" to a finished piece. They are also useful for breaking a bead - frequently the quickest and easiest way to remove a bead that has been woven in the wrong place.

Round nose pliers (curved on both inside and outside surface) can be used to form loops on the ends of wire findings, or for decorative wirework. The closer to the tip, the smaller the loop.

Flush cutting pliers are useful for cutting wire. Do not use these for cutting memory wire.

Diagonal cutting pliers where the outside (back) of the blades meets squarely, yielding a flat cut surface. The inside of the blades makes a pointed cut.

Chain Nose Pliers

Round Nose Pliers

Beeswax

Beeswax strengthens and protects your thread, and helps keep it from tangling. Before threading beads, run the thread through the beeswax, then pull the thread through your fingers to remove any excess wax. A thread conditioner called 'Thread Heaven' is also available.

Findings

Netted Beadwork

Netted beadwork is a fabric made up of beads and thread with one or more beads joined to a previous row, either thread to bead or thread to thread, and can be worked in almost any direction. The netting creates open spaces.

Definition of Terms

Beads that join two rows of beadwork will be referred to as 'shared beads' because they are shared between two rows and two threads. In this diagram they are the red beads. There are then connecting beads that connect to the shared beads. The completed sequence is called a 'loop'.

Perhaps the most common form of netted work is a 'three-bead netting' in which the netting is connected through the beads. You begin with a multiple of four beads, and then the second row is added by stringing three beads and going back through every fourth bead of the base row. The next rows are added by stringing on three beads and going though the centre bead of a three-bead loop in the previous row.

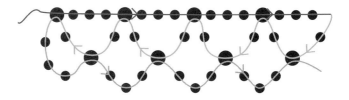

You are not restricted to just three beads. Loops can contain any number of beads as long as there are an odd number of beads in the loop (e.g. five, seven, nine).

To ensure that your netting lies flat, pass the needle through the shared bead so it is parallel to the thread already in the bead. Try not to pierce the previous thread.

Bead netting will stretch or sag in the opposite direction from which it was worked. For example, if the thread goes horizontally the work may stretch vertically.

Netted bead work can also be made by connecting between the beads by looping the thread around the thread between the beads of the previous row and then passing back through the last bead on the loop just added.

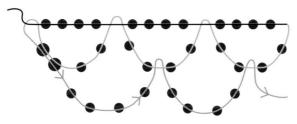

Edges for Flat Netting
There are many ways to work the edges of flat netting as shown below. Netting may have one style of edge on one side and another style on the other side.

Three bead netting with a flat edge

Three bead netting with a picot edge

Netted Beadwork

Increasing

You can increase by using more beads between the shared beads (areas of increase shown in green).

Decreasing

Connect shared beads with fewer or no connecting beads a the previous row.

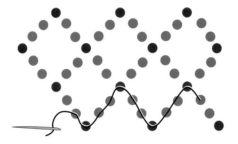

Peyote Stitch

Following Graphs

To follow a graph in an even or odd count flat peyote, work back and forth across each row, working down. To follow a graph in tubular peyote, work in a circle downward and at a diagonal. Each row will begin one bead over and one bead down from the previous row (step down). Peyote graphs can also be worked in brick stitch by turning 180 degrees.

Flat Peyote - Even Count
Step 1

Attach a stop bead to the thread, about 20cm from the end. Use a different size or style of bead for the 'stop' bead so you will not confuse it with the others.

stop bead

Step 2

Rows 1 and 2: String on the required amount of beads for the first two rows of the pattern (we will use 10 for descriptive purposes but these will vary according to the chart you are using). You can see on the diagram below that bead #1 will need to be the colour of the beads that you want in row two.

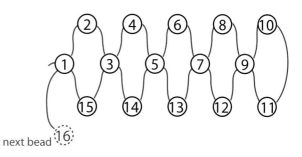

next bead

Step 3

Row 3: String on bead #11, pass the needle through bead #9. You are 'skipping' bead #10, the last bead strung. Continue to add beads #12 to #15.

Step 4

Row 4: Add bead #16, pass needle through bead #15. Hold the work carefully at this point as you do not want the beads to twist out of position. If the beads twist out of position, the pattern would not be correct and the twisted rows could cause problems with the tension. Continue adding beads #17 through to #20. Bead #20 is the last bead on row 4.

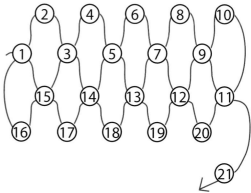

Step 5

Row 5: Add bead #21, passing needle through bead #20. Bead #21 is the first bead of row five. You will see how the rows line up with each other and the beads fit into each other, like a zipper's teeth. You will have 'down' beads that you go into when adding the next row. If you are using cylinder beads, this will be even more apparent.

Peyote Stitch

Flat Peyote - Odd Count
Odd count flat peyote is worked just the same as even count, but one side edge will be different.

Step 1
String on the required number of beads according to the chart you are working from (we will use 9 for descriptive purposes), using a 'stop' bead and proceed as even count flat peyote through to bead #13.

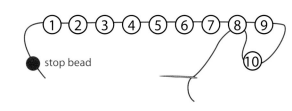

Step 2
From bead #13 go back through bead #2 and #1.

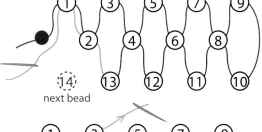

Step 3
String on bead #14 and go through bead #2 and #3, and pull bead into place.

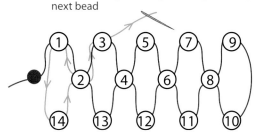

Step 4
Go through bead #13, #2 and #1 and back through #14. String on bead #15 and go through #13, and proceed as usual. In odd count flat peyote, one end will always be done as for even count peyote. The other end must be done as above for the first row.

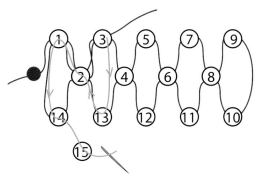

Increase Instructions

Step 1

To increase a row, you must work one row past the row you want to increase.

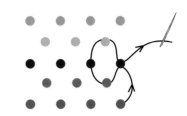

Step 2

Work to the blue row to begin the increase on the purple row. Add the increased bead on the purple row (the first row that you are increasing) and the first bead of the red row.

Step 3

Work your thread back up though the beads as shown: from the blue to the yellow, purple, green and out the yellow. This positions your thread to continue the second increased row, the red row.

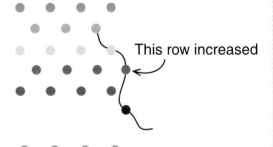

This row increased

Step 4

Work your thread back up though the beads as shown: blue, purple, green , yellow, purple. This positions your thread to continue the second increased row, the red row.

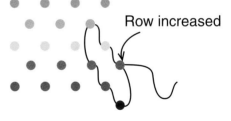

Row increased

Step 5

Take your thread back through the red bead and then the last blue bead. You can continue beading as normal.

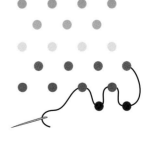

Peyote Stitch

Decrease Instructions

To decrease on the left side of a piece, simply 'skip' the bead by passing the thread back up through the last bead of the previous row and down through the second last bead of the row just worked. The thread is now in position to continue working the row as usual.

To decrease on the right side of the piece, you will do the same thing. Simply 'skip' the last bead by passing the thread through the last bead in the previous row and down through the second last bead of the row just worked. The thread is now in position to continue working the row as usual.

Remember if you have worked an increase or a decrease on one side only, you may have changed from an even count stitch to an odd count stitch, and will need to do the odd count turn at the end of the row.

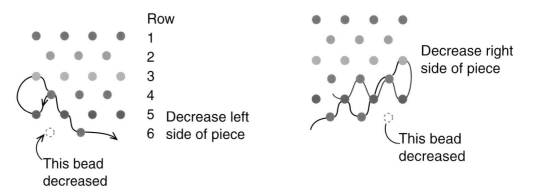

Row
1
2
3
4
5 Decrease left
6 side of piece

This bead
decreased

Decrease right
side of piece

This bead
decreased

Tubular Peyote

Working tubular peyote stitch is basically the same as flat peyote. The major difference is when you come back around to the first bead of the row. You will 'drop down' on the diagonal to begin the next row instead of turning your work or reversing directions as in flat peyote, always working from right to left and following the graph from the top to the bottom.

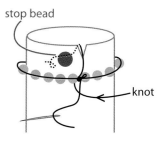

stop bead

knot

Using a Form

It is recommended that you use a 'form' to put the circle of beads on to work the piece. The form will help you keep consistent tension in the piece. A cardboard inner from a roll of cling wrap is great for this. Cut it lengthwise and push the roll together until it fits inside your bead circle. You may have to cut some of this if it rolls on itself too much. Tape the roll together, after making sure that it is straight and even all the way down. Do this by sliding the bead ring down along the tube as you tape. Go back and re-tape the whole length again, overlapping the tape to the inside of the roll on both ends. This will prevent you from snagging the thread on the tape as you work.

You can also cut a slit into the end of your tube and slip the end of your thread inside the tube.

Step 1

String on the required number of beads for the first two rows of the pattern (we will use 20 for descriptive purposes). Tie a circle, leaving about a one bead space, so the tension will not be too tight as you work the next row. Make certain that you have the bead circle facing the correct way. Take the needle back through the first bead strung to position the thread for the next row. You should be taking the thread to the left to add the next bead.

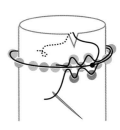

Step 2

Row 3: Pick up the first bead of row three (the red bead), skip a bead (the green bead) and put your needle through the second bead (the yellow bead).

Step 3

Pick up another bead, skip a bead and take the needle through the next bead. Continue until you get all the way around and cannot see where to put the next bead.

Peyote Stitch

Step 4

Pay attention to which was the first bead. After you add the last bead of the row you are working on, you must pass the thread through the first bead of that row to position the thread for the next row. You will have gone through two beads without adding a bead.

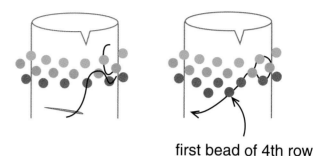

first bead of 4th row

Step 5

You will start the next row one bead over (and one bead down) from the start of the previous row. The starting point of each row is usually marked on the charts, and you can see how each row travels down the chart on the diagonal.

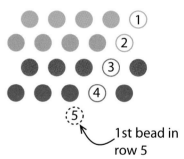

1st bead in row 5

Joining Seams ('zipper' seams)

To join a peyote stitch with a 'zipper' seam, make certain that you have worked the correct number of rows and that both the edges meet with the beads alternating on the sides so that they will interlock like a zipper. Take your thread through the first end bead, through the next bead that fits into the 'zipper' on the other side and continue this way, pulling on the thread every three to four beads. Do not pull too tight as it may warp your work.

Right Angle Weave is a type of bead weaving that forms rows of squares or crosses. The basic stitch is made up of four beads with sides that are at right angles to each other. As you learn this technique, you will be amazed at the variety of looks that can be achieved by modifying the stitch with different numbers and types of beads.

Instructions are given for two ways to construct the stitch, with two needles or with one needle. Try both methods and then proceed with the one you prefer.

Single Needle Right Angle Weave Instructions

Step 1
To begin single needle right angled weave, string four beads and pass back through all four beads again from the opposite side to form a circle. Tie the thread together between beads one and four to form a tight knot against the beads. Do not tie it too tightly, just use a firm tension. Beads make a cross or square.

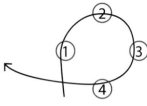

Step 2
Take the thread back through beads #1, #2 and #3.

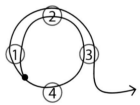

Step 3
Pick up beads #5, #6, and #7 and go back through bead #3 of the first square from the opposite direction to the thread. Pass though beads #5 and #6.

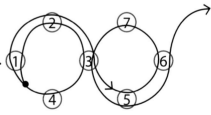

Step 4
Pick up three more beads and go back through bead #6 and the first two beads for the next square. Continue picking up three beads for each square until the row is the desired length.

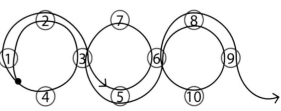

Step 5

To turn the corner and begin the second row, pass back through the last three beads of the last stitch of the first row and come out of side bead.

Step 6

Pick up three new beads and pass back through the side bead and the first new bead.

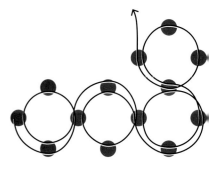

Step 7

From this point pick up two new beads for each square and pass back through the next side bead of the previous row and last bead of previous square.

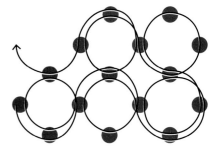

Step 8

The thread moves in a figure eight pattern. Do not cross horizontally or vertically between the squares.

Step 9

The thread path would be the same no matter how many beads you use per side. The stitch will always have four sides, but may have more than one bead per side.

Step 10

To increase length, make an extra square as shown in the diagram. The black line is the first pass and the blue line is the second pass. Turn the corner and proceed.

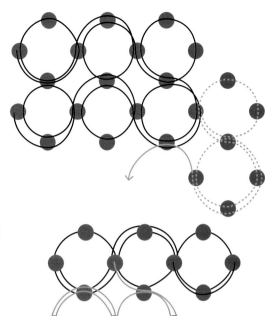

Step 11

To decrease a row by one square, follow the thread path shown in the diagram. The black line is the first pass and the blue line is the second pass. To decrease by more than one square, you will have to work back through the number of squares that you wish to decrease. Be sure to always follow the thread patterns and do not cross the open areas between the beads.

Double Needle Right Angle Weave Instructions

Step 1

Cut a length of thread and place a needle on each end. With one needle, pick up four beads and centre them on the thread. Take the second needle through the last bead picked up from opposite direction. Pull tight to make the first square.

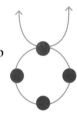

Step 2

Pick up one bead on first needle and 2 beads on the other needle. Take the first needle through the last bead on the second needle. Pull tight forming the second square. Continue in this manner until the row is one square short of the desired length.

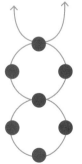

Right Angle Weave

Step 3

To make the last square of the first row, pick up 3 beads on one needle. Take the second needle though the last bead threaded and pull tight. Threads should be coming out of the side of the row.

Note: Threads should always be pointing in the direction you wish to bead.

Step 4

To start the second row, thread 3 beads on the needle closest to the ending of the piece of work. Take the other needle through the last bead from the opposite direction and pull tight.

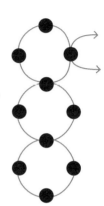

Step 5

You will now have one needle pointing in towards the work and one pointing out. Pass the needle pointing in through the side bead of the second square from the end of the first row and pull tight. Pick up two beads on the second needle. Take the first needle through last bead added and pull tight.

Step 6

Proceed down the row picking up two new beads each time and using side bead from the preceding row. Turn next corner.

Note: You are weaving figure eight patterns with the threads.

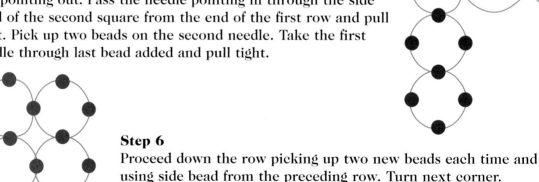

Step 7
To increase, weave the last square so the threads come out of the end bead. Pick up three new beads bringing thread out side bead and turn corner as usual. If you want to increase by more than one square, do the required squares and turn the corner or end the piece.

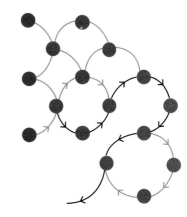

Step 8
To decrease by one square, bring threads out end bead and follow thread pattern shown in diagram. Continue down next row as usual. If you wish to decrease by more than one square, you will have to work the thread back through the piece to the place where the new square will start.

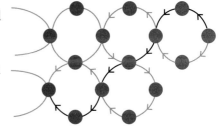

Step 9
To lay two pieces together for a pouch or cube, match point beads on two of the ends of the piece together. Centre the bead on the thread. Take each needle through the point beads on both sides and pull tight, pick up a bead on one needle and take the other needle through it from the opposite direction. Pull tight. Continue up the piece.

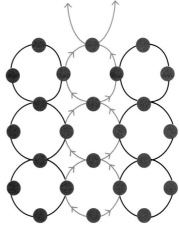

Right Angle Weave

Flower Necklace

Materials Needed
- Nymo beading thread
- Size 11 or 12 beading needle
- 5g of size 11 seed beads
- 4 mm bicones (or faceted beads)
- Clasp of choice

Step 1

Cut a piece a Nymo approximately 1.5m in length and thread the needle. Attach thread to clasp with three buttonhole stitches, leaving about a 5cm tail.

Step 2

Thread on 7 seed beads, *1 bicone, 1 seed bead, 1 bicone, 6 seed beads, and repeat from * until desired length is reached.

Step 3

Thread on one more seed bead and attach other end of clasp.

Continued over page...

Step 4
Pass back through the first seed bead from the clasp. Thread on 6 seed beads and 1 bicone. Pass the needle through the seed bead between the bicones.

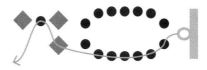

Step 5
Thread on 1 bicone, 6 seed beads 1 bicone and pass back through seed bead between bicones.

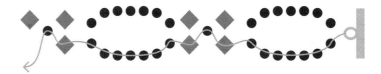

Step 6
Repeat Step 5 until the project is completed, ending the last repeat with 1 bicone and 6 seed beads.

Step 7
Pass the needle though the seed bead next to the clasp and do another buttonhole stitch around clasp.

Step 8
Pass back through completed work forming knots between the seed beads.

Tip
This technique can be applied to a necklace or bracelet.

Small Spike Necklace

Small Spike Necklace

Materials Needed
- 50g of main colour Size 9 seed beads
- 20g of contrast colour Size 9 seed beads
- Fine or medium beading thread
- Size 11 or 12 beading needle
- Necklace clasp of choice

Step 1

Fasten beading thread onto one end of the clasp with a couple of knots, and then three buttonhole stitches. Do not cut off the tail as this will be threaded under the beads before putting on the other end of the clasp.

Step 2

Thread on 1C (contrast bead,) 1M (main colour), *1C, 4M, repeat from * until almost length required allowing for the clasp, then thread 1C, 1M, 1C. Attach other end of the clasp, making sure to put tail under beginning beads, and that the beads are tight against the clasps. Fasten clasp with buttonhole stitches.

Step 3

First loop: Thread through to second contrast bead. Thread on 3C and form a loop, then pass through the first bead of this loop.

Step 4

Thread 3M, 1C, 4M, 2C, 1M, 1C, and form a loop at the base of the spike by passing the needle though the 4th bead from the needle. Thread on 4M, 1C, 3M and pass through contrast beads at top at opposite side of where you came down. Pass through 1C, 4M, 1C at top. Commence the second loop.

Step 5

Pick up 3C and form loop at top. Thread 3M, 1C, 4M, 2C, 1M, 1C and again form loop at base of spike. Now thread 4M and pass through first C from loop on the previous spike (see diagram). Thread 3M and pass through opposite side of first 3C loop and then again through base chain to next C bead.

To end the thread, pass the thread back through the necklace, making an occasional knot between the beads.

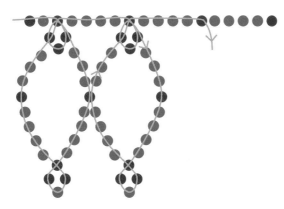

Striped Tubular Necklace

Materials Needed
- Nymo beading thread
- 20g each of two colours of size 11 seed beads
- Size 11 or 12 beading needle
- Clasp of choice

Step 1
Cut a piece a Nymo approximately 1.5m in length and thread the needle. Attach thread to clasp with three buttonhole stitches, leaving about a 5cm tail.

Step 2
Thread on 5 beads of the main colour and pass thread through the clasp. Repeat this twice. In the last five bead loop, pass through three beads so you are at the top of the loop.

Step 3
Thread on 5 beads of the second colour and pass the needle through the third (or central bead) of the next loop. Repeat this twice, and then pass through three beads in the first loop so that you are at the centre of the loop.

Step 4
Thread on 5 beads of the main colour and pass the needle through the third bead of the next loop. Repeat this twice, and then pass through three beads in the first loop so that you are at the centre of the loop.

Step 5
Repeat Steps 3 and 4 until you have reached the desired length, ending with Step 3. Pick up a main colour bead and pass through the centre bead of each of the three loops. Pass through this three main colour beads again and then pass through the other end of the clasp with four buttonhole stitches. End the thread off and pass it back though a few beads then knot and repeat this a couple of times. Cut off thread.

Tip

This technique can be applied to a necklace or bracelet.

Simple Pearl Necklace

Materials Needed
- Beading thread
- 50 of 6mm pearls (P) - for necklace
- Clasp of choice
- Extension chain

- Size 11 or 12 beading needle
- 2 bead tips
- 10g of size 11 seed beads (SB)
- Ear wires

Step 1
Cut a 2m length of thread for necklace and 1m for bracelet.
Thread a needle on each end.

Step 2
Thread on one seed bead (SB), and then pass both needles
through the bead tip with one length 1.5m and the other length
50cm for the necklace (70cm and 30cm for the bracelet). Close
bead tip around the seed bead.

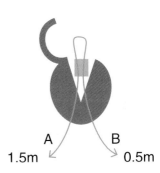

A   B

1.5m   0.5m

Step 3
On the longer length (A) thread on 5 SB, I pearl (P), 7 SB and
on the shorter length (B) thread on 5 SB, and then pass this
needle through the last 2 SB on A.

Step 4
On thread A thread on 5 SB, 1 P,
5 SB. On thread A thread on 7 SB.
Pass thread A through last 2 SB
on thread B.

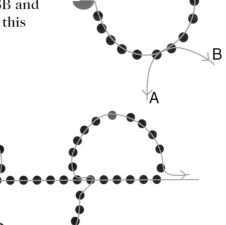

Continued over page...

Simple Pearl Necklace

Step 5
Repeat Step 4 until you reach the required length (approximately 49 pearls for the necklace).

Step 6
On the last repeat thread B has only 5 SB and thread A has 5 SB, 1 P, 5 SB. Pass both needles through a bead tip and thread a SB on one thread. Tie a series of knots and glue. Cut off thread and close bead tip.

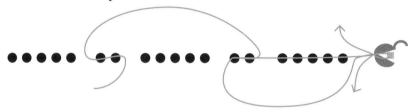

Step 7
Attach findings. An extension chain is a useful way of finishing off necklaces if you wish to alter the length. For the bracelet just attach the clasp.

Earrings
Step 1
Cut a 20cm length of thread and thread a needle at each end with 15cm and 5cm. Complete as per diagram and attach ear wire of choice.

Tip
This technique can be applied to a necklace, bracelet or earrings.

Petal Necklace

Petal Necklace

Materials Needed
- Beading thread
- Approx. 100 of 4mm bicones (BC)
- 10g of size 11 seed beads (SB)
- Size 11 or 12 beading needle
- Clasp of choice

Step 1
Cut a 1.5m length of thread and thread a needle on each end.

Step 2
Thread on 4 seed beads (SB), one end of the clasp, 3 SB, 1 bicone bead (BC) and pass the needle back through first seed bead to form a loop.

Step 3
On the upper needle, thread on 6 SB and on the lower needle thread, on 1 BC and pass this needle through the last bead on the other needle.

Step 4
Repeat Step 3.

Step 5
On the lower needle, thread on 6 SB and on the upper needle thread on a bicone and pass this needle through the last bead on the other needle.

Step 6
Repeat Step 5 twice.

Step 7
Continue as set in pattern reversing sequence of beads after three repeats, until you reach the required length.

Step 8
At the last repeat, thread 3 SB other end of clasp and then 3 SB and then weave the ends through the completed work.

Tip
This technique can be applied to a necklace or bracelet.

Petal Necklace

Cleopatra Necklace

Materials Needed
• 20g of size 9 seed beads (Main colour - MC)
• 5g of size 9 seed beads (Contrast colour - CC)
• Size 11 or 12 beading needle
• Beading thread
• Clasp of choice

Step 1
Attach clasp to thread with 5 - 6 buttonhole stitches around one
end of the clasp and leave a 10cm tail. Pass thread through the
clasp and then through the loop formed by the thread.

Step 2
Thread on 1 CC, 1 MC, *1 CC, 4 MC, and repeat from * until you reach the length
required. Thread on 1 CC, 1 MC, 1 CC, slide beads over the tail at the clasp end of
the thread and then attach the other end of the clasp.

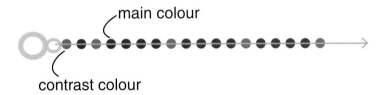

main colour

contrast colour

Step 3
Pass needle through 1 CC, 1 MC, 1 CC ready to begin the first loop.

Continued over page...

Cleopatra Necklace

Step 4

Thread on 3 CC and pass back through the same contrast bead on the base to form a loop, and then back through the first bead just added.

Step 5

Thread on 3 MC, 1 CC, 4 MC, 1 CC, 5 MC, 2 CC, 1 MC, 1 CC and pass back through the 4th bead from the needle to form a picot.

Step 6

Thread on 5 MC, 1 CC, 4 MC, and pass through the first CC on the loop.

Step 7
Thread on 3 MC beads and pass through the other side of the original three bead loop and then through 1 CC, 4 MC, 1 CC on base.

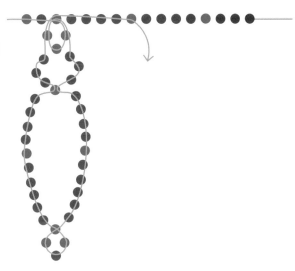

Step 8
Repeat Step 4 and 5

Step 9
Thread on 5 MC and pass through the contrast bead on the adjoining loop.

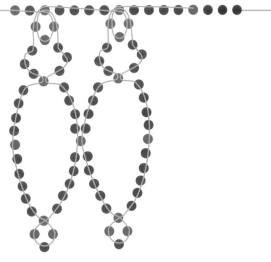

Step 10
Repeat steps 6 and 7.

Step 11
Repeat Steps 8, 9 and 10 until you reach the end of the base beads. To finish off the thread, weave back through the loops forming the occasional knot between the beads.

Cleopatra Necklace

Spiral Twist Necklace

Materials Needed
• Beading thread
• Size 11 or 12 beading needle
• 10g of size 11 seed beads main colour (MC)
• 5g of size 11 seed beads contrast colour (CC)
• Clasp of choice

Step 1
Cut a 2m length of thread and thread a needle. Thread on 3 MC, 1 end of the clasp, 3 MC and pass back through all of these to form a circle. Tie a couple of knots. Pass back through the circle again to strengthen it.

Step 2
Thread on enough MC beads until you reach the length required having a multiple of three beads. Thread on 3 MC the other end of the clasp, 3 MC and again pass through all these so that they form a circle. Pass through the circle again to strengthen it.

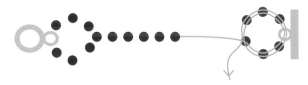

Step 3
Thread on 3 MC and pass through the 3rd bead from the clasp circle. Repeat this until you reach the other end of the base bead chain. Your work will start to spiral at this stage.

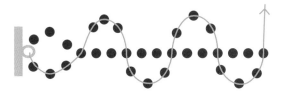

Continued over page...

Spiral Twist Necklace

Step 4

When you reach the end, pass through the clasp circle again and then through the first two beads of the last three bead loop added.

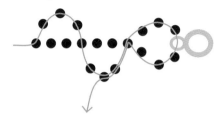

Step 5

Thread on 5MC and pass though the middle bead of the next three bead loop. Repeat this until you reach the end of the three bead loops. Thread on three beads and pass back through the middle bead of the last five bead loop added.

Step 6

Thread on 7 CC beads and pass through the middle bead of the next five bead loop. Repeat until you reach the last five bead loop. End the thread by weaving it back through the completed work.

Tip

This technique can be applied to a necklace or bracelet.

Three Tone Netted Amulet Bag

Three Tone Netted Amulet Bag

Materials Needed
- 10g of size 11 beads main colour (MC)
- 5g of size 11 beads contrast 1 (C1)
- 5g of size 11 beads contrast 2 (C2)
- Beading thread
- Size 10-12 beading needle
- 36 Bugle beads to match one of the colours used (extra if using them in strap)

Step 1
Work the neck with 36 bugle beads and 2m of thread. A long thread will ensure that the thread will work all of the bugle beads, and some of the net without a join. If threads have to be joined whilst working the neck, the holes in the bugle beads will get full of thread. The holes need to be free to attach the net to the neck.

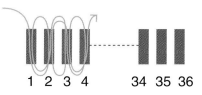

You can make the purse wider or narrower by using more or less bugle beads in the neck. If you decide to change the number of bugle beads in the neck, then keep to an even number of beads, as you need two beads in the neck to complete the two rows that make up each net. Complete the neck but do not join it up into a circle at this stage. The purse is worked flat and joined into a circle when the netting is finished.

Step 2
Using the thread left from working the neck, pick up 6 beads in the following sequence 1C1, 2MC, 1C2, 2MC. Repeat this sequence until you have 36 beads on the thread. If you wish to make the purse longer you must add more round beads in multiples of six. The number of beads, six, applies to five-bead netting.

Step 3
Once you have 36 beads on your thread, pull them up close to the bugle bead. Count back 12 beads - the 25th bead from the top (a C1 in this case) - and pass the needle through it. Pull the thread gently so that the beads form a loop.

Step 4

Keeping the colours correct, in this instance starting with a MC bead, add 5 more beads (2MC, 1 C2, 2MC). Take the needle through the 19th bead. The loop should always join through a contrast bead.

Step 5

Continue adding 5 beads (2MC, 1C2) 2MC) and work the thread through the 6th bead back along the thread until you arrive at the 1st bead in the line.

Step 6

Take the needle up through the next bugle bead and down through the bugle bead next to it. You have now completed the two rows that make a net. To keep the tension even, lay the work on a flat surface, and then pull the thread up through the first connecting bead.

Step 7

Add 3 more beads (1C1, 2 MC). Take the needle through the 4th bead (C2) of the previous row of netting. This is the middle contrast bead of the previous five bead net. Add five beads in the following order (2MC, 1C1, 2MC) and work through the centre bead of the previous net. Repeat this process until you reach the last connecting bead.

Continued over page...

Three Tone Netted Amulet Bag

Step 8

Add 8 beads (2MC, 1C1, 2MC, 1C2, 2MC) and work through the 12th bead back. Continue adding five beads in the correct colours until you reach the bugle beads.

Step 9

Go through the next bugle bead and down through the one next to it. You are now ready to add three more beads to start the next row of netting.

Step 10

Continue the netting until you reach the 2nd last bugle bead. Work to the bottom of the purse as usual, but only add 5 beads instead of 8 (2MC, 1C1, 2MC) at the end of the row. Fold the pure so that the two edges are close to one another, and work out which are the joining beads in the first and last rows. Take the needle through the joining bead (C2) of the outer edge of the purse.

Step 11

Add 2MC beads, and pick up the joining bead (C1) from the other edge following the dotted red line. Continue adding 2 beads and joining the edges all the way up the purse, following the dotted red line.

Step 12

After working the last round bead at the top, take the needle up through the last bugle bead on one edge of the purse and down through the first bugle bead of the other edge. Repeat this as many times as you can. Do not cut thread. You now have a circular net purse with a hole at the bottom, which has to be joined.

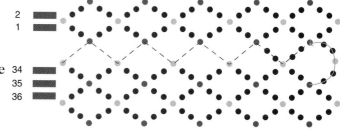

Step 13

Fold the purse flat so that the points of the net at the bottom are on top of one another. Avoid placing the join in the bugle beads at either side of the purse.

Netting is open work, so any thread that crosses a space will show. The threads must follow the course of the netting.

Step 14

Take the thread at the bugle beads through the netting to the corner join at the bottom of the purse, at the right hand side, through the last joining bead. Go through the bead at the back of the purse, across again and through the bead at the front. Take the thread through the netting to the next connecting point. Continue until the bottom of the purse is joined.

Step 15

When you have connected the last pair of common beads, secure the thread by working back through the netting, and take it up to the point where you wish to begin the strap. You can make your own design for the strap, or follow the sequence provided.

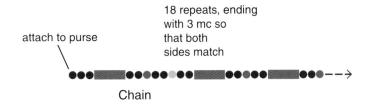

attach to purse

18 repeats, ending with 3 mc so that both sides match

Chain

Netted Lariat Choker

Materials Needed
• Fine or extra fine beading thread
• Size 11 or 12 beading needle
• 10g of size 11 seed beads main colour (MC)
• 10g of size 11 seed beads contrast colour (CC)
• Feature beads for dangles if required

Step 1

Cut a length of thread and thread a needle. Secure a CC bead leaving a tail. Add 5 beads in the following order, 1MC, 1CC, 2MC, 1CC. Turn and work back through the 2nd bead back (the 1st MC). The first bead acts as a stop bead.

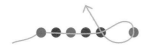

Step 2

Add 3 beads (1MC, 1CC, 1MC). Work through the first bead that you picked up, the one with the tail hanging from it.

Step 3

Pick up 2M, 1CC. Turn back and work through the middle bead that you have just added.

Continued over page...

Step 4

Add 3 beads (1MC, 1CC, 1MC) and work through the middle bead of the three bead loop (the green bead) which appears to be the middle of the diamond. This is the green bead.

Step 5

Add 3 beads (2MC, 1CC) and work back through the first MC bead.

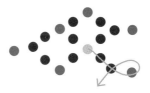

Step 6

Add (1MC, 1CC, 1MC) and work through the yellow bead. You should be able to see a pattern emerging. This is continued by adding (2MC, 1CC), working back through the first MC bead, then adding another 3 beads (1MC, 1CC, 1MC) to complete the off-centre diamond between each side. Repeat until you reach the desired length. For a lariat it is about 1.2m.

Tip

This technique can be applied to a choker or bracelet.

Crystal Choker

Crystal Choker

Materials Needed
- Approx. 300 of 4mm crystals
- 16 seed beads to match crystals
- Size 10-12 beading needle
- Nymo D beading thread
- Clasp of your choice
- Extension chain

Step 1
Thread needle with approximately 1.5m of beading thread. Thread on 1 crystal, 4 seed beads, clasp, 4 seed beads and pass back through the crystal. Pass back through the seed beads, clasp and seed beads to reinforce the clasp, and tie a knot with the starting tail. Pass through the crystal.

Step 2
Pick up three crystals and pass back through the first crystal, passing the needle from the opposite side from where the thread is coming from. This should form a square with the four beads. Then pass back through two of the crystals just added so that you are back at the base of the square.

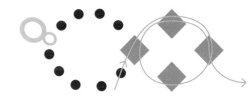

Step 3
Repeat step 2 until the choker is about 2 squares longer than the required length as the next rows will tighten your work.

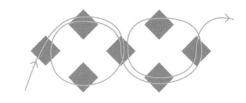

Step 4

Pass the thread through the last square so that the thread is coming out of one of the side beads. Pick up 3 crystals and pass back through the crystal from the other side from where the thread is coming from. Pass back through three crystals from this square and the first side crystal of the next square.

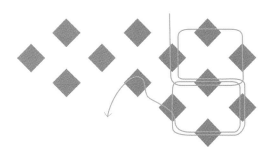

Step 5

Continue picking up 2 crystals and complete right angle weave as per instructions.

Step 6

When you reach the end of this side thread through to side bead on other side of middle crystal and complete other side to match.

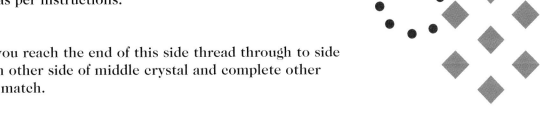

Step 7

When you reach the end of the choker check the length again as the working of the side rows will have tightened up your work. If it is too short, add more rows to the end. Attach extension chain in the same manner as Step 1 starting from the centre square.

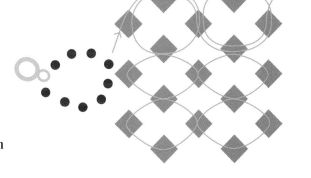

Step 8

Finish off threads by weaving them through the completed work, tying knots over the threads between the beads.

Tip

This technique can be applied to a choker or bracelet.

Crystal Choker

Grace Crystal Necklace

Materials Needed
- Beading thread
- Approx. 80 of 4mm bicones (BC)
- 5g of size 11 seed beads (C1)
- Clasp of choice

- Size 11 or 12 beading needle
- 10g of size 11 seed beads (MC)
- 2 bead tips

Step 1
Cut a 2m length of thread and thread a needle on each end. Cut a 1m length and thread a needle on one end.

Step 2
Knot the 1m length around a SB. Pass one end of the longer thread through the same SB and centre the bead on the thread. Pass all three threads though a bead tip. Close bead tip around bead. Set the single thread aside.

Step 3
On one thread place 1 SB and pass other needle through in the opposite direction.

Step 4
On each thread place 4 MC, 1 C, 4 MC. On one thread place one extra MC and then pass the other thread through this bead from the opposite direction to form a circle.

Continued over page...

Grace Crystal Necklace

Grace Crystal Necklace

Step 5

Now on each thread place 1 MC, 1 C, 1 MC.
On one thread place an extra MC and then
pass other thread through bead from the
opposite direction to form a circle.

Step 6

Repeat Steps 4 and 5 until you reach the required length ending with a large circle.
Do not cut threads.

Step 7

With the third thread pass through 4 MC, 1C on the
first loop.

Step 8

Thread on 4 MC, 4 BC and pass thread back though
first BC.

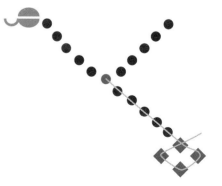

Step 9
Thread on 4 MC and pass though C on second loop on base.

Step 10
Repeat Step 9 until you reach the last large circle.

Step 11
Pass thread through 5 MC beads on large circle.

Step 12
Pass all three threads through a bead tip and then two of these threads through a seed bead. Knot firmly and seal knots. Close bead tip around bead.

Step 13
Attach clasp of choice.

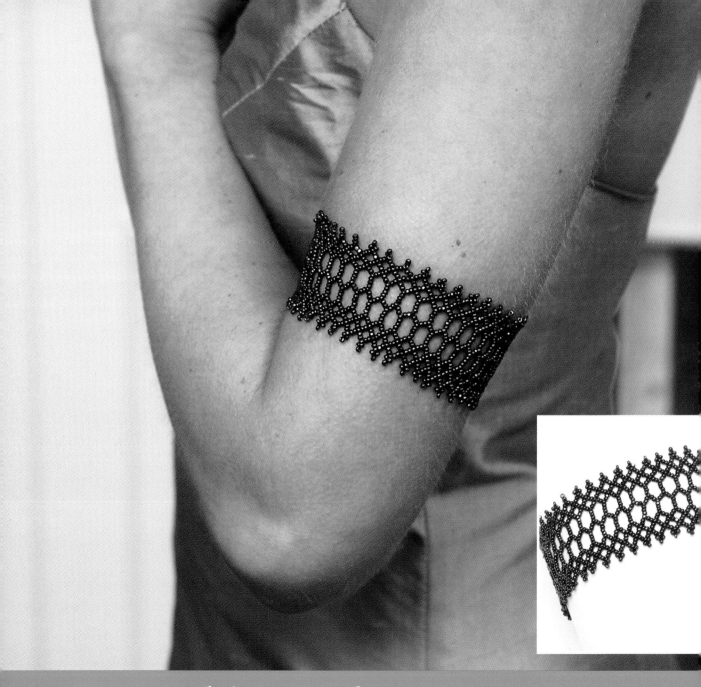

Hexagonal Arm Band

Materials Needed
- 20g of size 11 seed beads
- Size 10-12 beading needle
- Beading thread

Step 1
String on one bead. Form two buttonhole stitches over this bead to secure it in place. Leave about a 10cm tail, which will be woven into the beads to conceal it once the bracelet is completed.

Step 2
String on 29 more beads (30 beads in total). Pass back through the 4th bead from the needle (for example, bead 27) to form a picot.

Step 3
String on 5 beads and pass back through the 6th bead (for example, bead 21).

Step 4
String on 9 beads, skip 9 beads on the base length and pass back through the next 5 beads.

Continued over page...

Step 5
String 5 beads, skip 5 beads, and pass back through the 6th bead (for example, bead no 1).

Step 6
String on 6 beads. Pass back through the 4th bead from the needle to form a picot on the end.

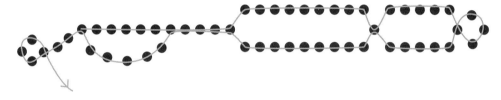

Step 7
Repeat Steps 2 to 5 until you reach your desired length. You will always pass through the middle bead or beads of the previous row's loop. There are always two beads between each joined beads.

Step 8

To complete the bracelet, weave the netting until it is long enough to fit snugly over your knuckles when stretched slightly. Lay the piece flat and fold the bracelet so that the ends meet. These should lock together like a jigsaw. If not, add or take off a row of beading. Weave the two pieces together to form a completed circle. The red beads in the diagram below are the beads added to weave the two ends together.

Step 9

When completed, weave the ends through the bead nets forming the occasional knot between the beads.

Tip

This technique can be applied to an arm band or bracelet.

Ophelia Necklace

Materials Needed
- Beading thread
- Size 11 or 12 beading needle
- Approx. 200 of 4mm pearls
- 20g of size 11 seed beads (SB)
- 2 bead tips
- Clasp of choice

Step 1
Cut two 2m lengths of thread and thread a needle on each end of both threads so you end up with four needles.

Step 2
Pass two threads through a bead and then all four threads through a bead tip.

Step 3
Close bead tip.

Step 4
Thread 3 SB on each pair of threads and then pass one pair of threads through a pearl (P).

Step 5
Work right angle weave with pearls and centre threads until the length required, but do not cut thread. Set these threads aside.

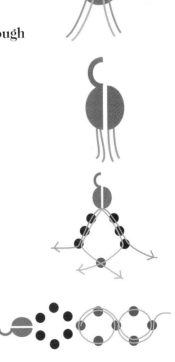

Continued over page...

Step 6

Thread on 10 SB on each needle on the outer threads.

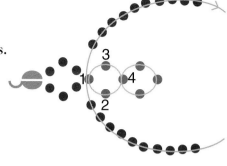

Step 7

Pass thread A through Pearl #3 back towards clasp. Pass thread B through Pearl #2 back towards clasp.

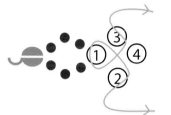

Step 8

Thread on 7 SB on each thread and pass through Pearl #4 from opposite directions.

Step 9

Repeat Step 7 and 8 until you reach the end.

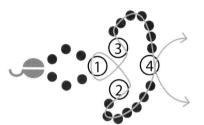

Step 10

Pass all threads though the final pearl and then on each pair of threads thread on 3 SB. Pass all four threads through a bead tip and then a pair of threads through a bead. Knot off and seal the knot. Close the bead tip around the SB.

Step 11

Attach clasp to each end of the necklace.

Tip

This technique can be applied to a necklace or bracelet.

Peyote Triangle Bracelet

Materials Needed
- Beading thread
- Size 11 or 12 beading needle
- 1 packet of each of Delica in three contrasting colours C1, C2, C3
- Clasp of choice

Step 1
Cut a long length of thread and thread a needle. Attach a stopper bead by passing through this bead twice, but leaving a 20cm tail. Pick up 10 C1 beads, as per graph.

Step 2
Following graph as set out, work even count peyote. For the third row you will pick up 5 C1 beads.

Row 4: 1C2, 4C1
Row 5: 4C1, 1 C2
Row 6: 2C2, 3C1
Row 7: 3C1, 2C2
Row 8: 3C2, 2C1
Row 9: 2C1, 3C2
Row 10: 4C2, 1C1
Row 11: 1C1, 4C2
Row 12: 5C2
Row 13: 5C2
Row 14: 4C2, 1C3
Row 15: 1C3, 4C2
Row 16: 3C2, 2C3
Row 17: 2C3, 3C2
Row 18: 2C2, 3C3
Row 19: 3C3, 2C2
Row 20: 1C2, 4C3
Row 21: 4C3, 1C2
Row 22: 5C3
Row 23: 5C3

Step 3
Continue as set out, alternating colours as triangles are completed.

Step 4
Decrease each end down to one bead and attach clasp of choice.

Tip
This technique can be applied to a bracelet or choker.

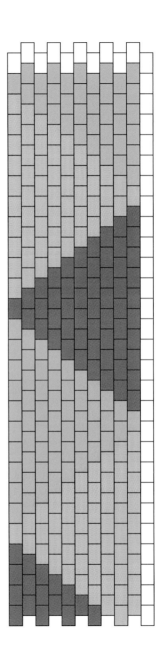

Peyote Triangle Bracelet

Beaded Bead Necklace

Materials Needed
- Small amount of Delica beads in a variety of colours
- Beading thread
- Size 10-12 beading needle
- Clasp of you choice

This is a great project to use up any small amounts of beads left over from larger projects. A beaded bead is simply a strip of flat peyote sewn together to make a tube.

Step 1

Following the instructions for flat even count peyote, work a 10 bead wide by 10 row strip.

Step 2

'Zip' the seam and you have a bead to string.

Step 3

Work a variety of beads in different colours and sizes (for example, 10 x 10, 8 x 10, 6 x 10, 12 x 10).

Step 4

Attach a clasp to end of a length of thread. Thread on 10 black Delica beads, a beaded bead, 6 black Delica beads, another beaded bead, and repeat until you reach the required length. Attach the other end of the clasp and finish off the thread.

Tip

This technique can be applied to a necklace or bracelet.

Flower Trail Bracelet

Materials Needed
- Beading thread
- Size 11 or 12 beading needle
- Delica beads in colour of choice
- Delica beads in colour of choice
- 2 pkts of background colour
- 1 pkt of each of the design colours
- Clasp of choice

Step 1
Cut a long length of thread and thread a needle. Attach a stopper bead by passing through this bead twice, but leaving a 20cm tail.

Step 2
Following graph set out, work rows 1-25. The pattern repeat is rows 12-25. Keep working these rows until you reach the required length.

pattern repeat

Step 3
Decrease each end down to one bead and attach clasp of choice.

Tip
This technique can be applied to a bracelet or choker.

Blooms Earrings

Materials Needed
- Beading thread
- Size 11 or 12 beading needle
- Delica beads in colour of choice
    - 2 pkts of background colour
    - 1 pkt of each of the design colours
- Clasp of choice

Step 1

Cut a long length of thread and thread a needle. Attach a stopper bead by passing through this bead twice, but leaving a 20cm tail. Pick up 9 background colour beads, as per graph.

Step 2

Following the graph, work rows 1-27. This is odd count peyote, so there will be the figure-of-eight turn as described in the peyote instructions at the end of every second row. The pattern repeat is rows 5-27. Keep working these rows until you reach the required length.

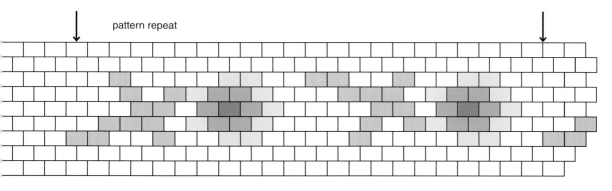

pattern repeat

Step 3

Decrease each end down to one bead, and attach clasp of choice.

Tip

This technique can be applied to a choker, bracelet or earrings.

Peyote Amulet Bag

Materials Needed

- 20g of Delica beads main colour • 10g of Delica beads contrast colour
- Beading thread   • Size 10-12 beading needle
- Cardboard support roll (inner of cling wrap roll)
- 26 of 4mm crystals to match main colour (for dangles if required)
- 13 of 4mm crystals to match contrast colour (for dangles if required)
- 12 of dagger beads (for dangles if required)

This bag is worked in even-count and odd-count peyote, incorporating both flat and tubular peyote.

A ruler placed on the chart will help when reading the rows. Remember that the rows 'stack' up one half bead. Note: the first bead of every row will be one more bead to the left. The amulet bag graph is charted flat however it will be worked in a tubular peyote stitch. Refer to the general peyote instructions for placements of the row.

Tubular peyote for the body of the bag (using a cardboard cling wrap roll as a support tube).

Step 1

Thread a beading needle with 150cm of thread and pick up 50 main colour beads. Tie threads together with a square knot to form a circle.

Step 2

Cut cardboard support tube length-wise and push roll together, making sure that it is straight all the way up. Tape it when it is the size to fit within the ring of 50 beads. Slip the ring of beads over the support tube and adjust beads.

Step 3

Refer to pattern graph. Start from the bottom of the pattern. Take the needle through the first bead, then *pick up a bead, skip a bead and go through the next bead, pull up tight. Repeat from * to end of row. When ending the row, pass needle through the first bead of row 2 and the first bead of row 3.

Continued over page...

Step 4

Refer to the tubular peyote stitch diagram and continue the above process as set in the graph to complete the body of the bag. End all loose threads by weaving through the rows diagonally to secure. Cut thread close to work.

Step 5

Bag flap (flat and odd count peyote techniques)

Remove body of bag from support tube. Squeeze bag flat so that the pattern appears in the middle of the front of the bag.

Step 6

Work flat peyote stitch for 8 rows as per graph and then decrease first and last bead of every row until one bead remains. You can now end the thread or weave it through to the position where you wish to commence the strap.

Step 7

Strap (even count flat peyote)

Pick up a bead and weave into the first 'down beads' on the graph. Continue working 4 beads across to make the strap (for example, adding two beads per row) until you reach the length required. Butt together the second side of the bag and the end of the strap to form a zipper. If beads do not interlock add another row of beads. Weave together through interlocking beads.

Step 8

To close the bottom of the bag, take thread to bottom of the bag and weave through the interlocking beads (for example, the first rows done).

Step 9

Fringe

This is a V-shaped fringe with 13 sets of dangles. Thread on 1.5m of beading thread and attach to bottom of the bag, at one end of the bag. Pick up beads as per diagram and then return the needle up through the beads, starting with the last 4mm faceted bead. Be careful not to split the thread when going up through the beads a second time. Continue the V-shaping as per the fringe diagram. When complete, end thread by weaving back through the body of the bag.

Box Bracelet With Oversew

Materials Needed
- 80 of 4mm crystals
- Size 10-12 beading needle
- Clasp of your choice
- 1 pkt of Delica beads in contrasting colour
- Nymo D beading thread

Step 1
Thread needle with approximately 1.5m of beading thread.
Thread on 1 crystal, 4 Delica beads, clasp, 4 Delica beads
and pass back through the crystal. Pass back through the
Delica beads, clasp and Delica beads to reinforce the clasp
and tie a knot with the starting tail. Pass through the crystal.

Step 2
Pick up three crystals and pass back through the first crystal,
passing the needle from the opposite side from where the
thread is coming from. This should form a square with the
four beads. Then pass back through two if the crystals just
added so that you are back at the base of the square.

Step 3
Repeat step 2 until the bracelet is about 2 squares
longer than the required length as the oversew will
tighten your work.

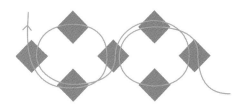

Continued over page...

Box Bracelet With Oversew

Step 4

You are now at the centre bead of the last square. Thread on 4 Delica beads, the other end of the clasp, 4 Delica beads and pass back through the crystal from the other side from where the thread is coming from. Pass back through Delica beads, clasp, Delica beads and crystal again to reinforce the clasp.

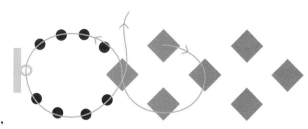

Step 5

Now pick up 5 Delica beads and pass through the middle crystal on the next loop so that the Delicas are across the square. Your thread will be following a 'Z trail'. Repeat this step until you get to the end of the bracelet.

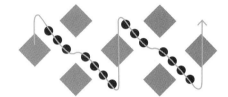

Step 6

Now take the thread through first middle bead of square and pick up 2 Delica beads. Pass through the 3rd bead of the five already crossing the box, then pick up another 2 Delica beads and pass through the middle crystal again. This should form an 'X' between the crystals. Repeat this until you get to the other end of the bracelet. Tie off thread and hide the ends.

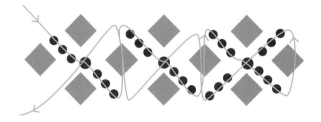

Bella Necklace

Bella Necklace

Materials Needed
- Approx. 190 of 4mm crystals (C4)
- Size 10-12 beading needle
- Clasp of your choice
- Approx. 200 of 6mm crystals (C6)
- Nymo D beading thread
- 2mm beads

Step 1
Cut a length of thread approximately 2m long and thread a needle at each end. Pick up 1 C6 and 3C4 and centre them on the thread. Take the needle through the last C4 added to form a circle.

Step 2
Thread on 1C6 on the same side as previous and 2C4 on the other needle. Pass the needle from the C6 through the last C4 added.

Step 3
Repeat Step 2 until you have completed 9 squares. Thread 1C6 on one needle and 1 C4 on the other needle and pass both needles through the C4 at the base square to complete a circle, with all the C6 in the outside.

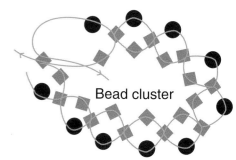

Bead cluster

Step 4
Thread through so that both needles are coming from opposite sides of a C6 bead in the circle.

Step 5
Thread on one needle 3C4 and on the other needle 1C6 and then pass this needle through the last C4 added.

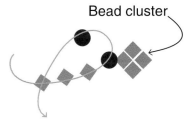

Bead cluster

Step 6

Repeat Step 5 once and then change the sequence of beads added so that the C6 is now on the opposite needle to previous.

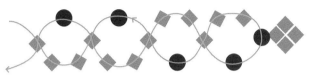

Step 7

Continue this sequence until you reach the length required and then attach the clasp and finish off the thread by weaving though the completed side.

Step 8

Cut a length of thread and thread a needle on both ends. Pass a needle through the second C6 on the circle from the one from which the other strap is coming from. Complete other strap as previously and attach chain. Finish off one of the threads.

Step 9

With the thread remaining weave back through the C4 beads at the side of the strap adding a 2mm bead between them. Continue around the circle in the same manner, and then up the other side of the strap. End off thread by weaving through the completed work.

Step 10

When you reach the end of this side, thread through to side bead on other side of middle crystal and complete other side to match.

Step 11

When you reach the end of the choker check the length again as the working of the side rows will have tightened up your work. If it is too short, add more rows to the end. Attach extension chain in the same manner as Step 1, starting from the centre square.

Step 12

Finish off threads by weaving them through the completed work, tying knots over the threads between the beads.

Waves Necklace

Materials Needed
- Beading thread
- Size 11 or 12 beading needle
- 20g of size 11 seed beads main colour (MC)
- 20g of size 11 seed beads contrast colour (CC)
- Clasp of choice

Step 1
Cut a 2m length of thread and thread a needle at both ends of the thread. Attach to clasp of choice and then pass both needles in opposite directions through a seed bead.

Step 2
Form a right angle weave base with the MC beads until you reach the length required plus an extra 3cm. Attach other end of the clasp.

Step 3
Working with one needle at a time, weave back through the base to the beginning, and then repeat with the other needle but working on other side of squares.

Continued over page...

Step 4

Tie a series of knots and end off one of these threads. Pass the remaining thread back through the beads so that it is coming out of the bottom bead of square and facing the clasp.

Step 5

Pick up 5 MC, 5 CC, 5 MC and pass through second bottom bead on base length so that the needle is pointing towards the clasp.

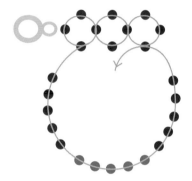

Step 6

Pick up 5 MC, 6 CC, 5 MC and pass through the second bottom bead on base length so that the needle is pointing towards the clasp.

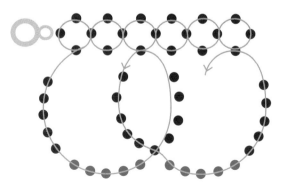

Step 7
Repeat Step 6 increasing one CC bead each loop until you reach the centre of the base length. Work the centre loop.

Step 8
Turn the work over and, working from the back, repeat Step 6 decreasing one CC bead until you reach the end with the last repeat being 5 MC, 5 CC, 5 MC. By turning over your work it looks like all the loops are sitting behind the centre loop.

Step 9
Finish off your thread within the loops.

Beaded Lace Choker

Materials Needed

- 20g of size 11 seed beads
- Size 10-12 beading needle
- 1 of 6mm wooden bead
- Nymo D beading thread

Step 1

Cut a length of thread approximately 1.5m long and thread a needle at one end. Pick up 10 beads and pass back through them so that they form a circle. Tie a couple of knots and then pass through six beads.

Step 2

Pick up 8 beads and pass back through last 2 beads on previous square. Thread through 6 beads so that you are at the base of the square.

Step 3

Repeat Step 2 until you have reached the required length.

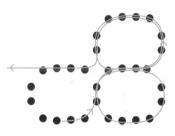

Step 4

Turn the work around and thread through 4 beads so that you are at the side of the square. Add eight beads and pass back through the 4 side beads and then through 2 base beads.

Step 5

Continue adding 6 beads to complete the squares down the side of the original row.

Continued over page...

Beaded Lace Choker

Step 6

When you reach the end, pass through to the centre beads and thread on 58 beads. Pass back through the 30th bead from needle to form a loop.

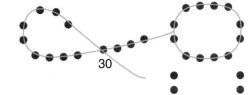

Step 7

Thread on 14 beads, miss 14 beads and pass through the next bead. Thread on 14 beads and pass through the middle bead of the other square on the base. Pass back through all these beads twice more to strengthen.

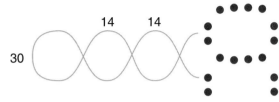

Step 8

Thread through the 2 beads across the top of the square and then through 2 beads on the side. Thread on 12 beads. Miss one square and pass thread between the middle of the four bead side of the next square. Pass thread back through the first bead.

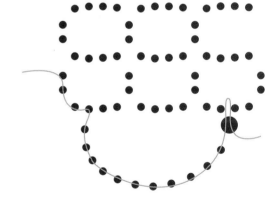

Step 9

Thread on 11 beads, miss one square and pass thread between middle of next four bead side. Continue until you reach the end.

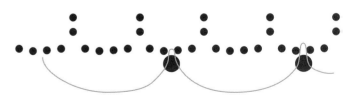

Step 10

Pass through to centre of end square and thread on 26 beads. Pass thread through wooden bead. Thread on enough beads (approximately 8 beads) to cover wooden bead and pass back through the bead. Repeat until the entire bead is covered.

Step 11

Pass back through last bead before wooden bead. Thread on 12 beads, miss 12 beads and pass through next bead. Thread on 12 beads and pass through centre bead on other square. Pass back through all these beads to reinforce.

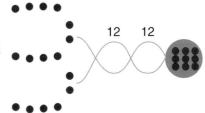

Step 12

Repeat Step 8 and then Step 9 until you reach the other end. Finish off the thread by weaving through the completed work.

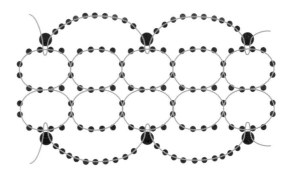

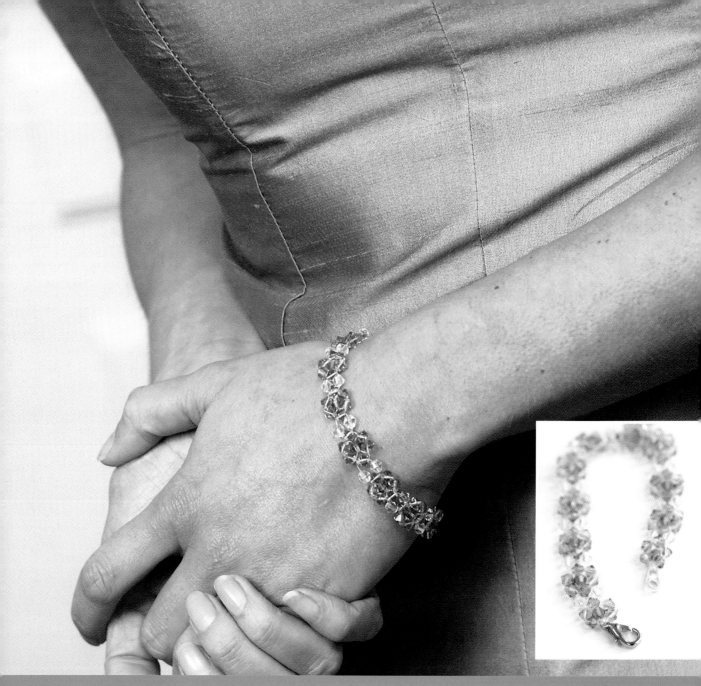

Block Flower Bracelet

Materials Needed
- Beading thread
- Size 11 or 12 beading needle
- Approx. 64 of 4mm bicones (Main Colour MC)
- Approx. 11 of 4mm bicones (1st contrast C1)
- Approx. 20 of 4mm bicones (2nd contrast C2)
- Clasp of choice

Step 1
Cut a 1.5m length of thread and thread a needle on each end.

Step 2
Pass one needle through the clasp and centre the clasp on the thread. Attach firmly with a series of knots.

Step 3
Pick up 2 MC beads on each needle.

Step 4
Pick up one C1 bead and pass both needles through it in the same direction.

Step 5
Pass a needle back up through the two MC beads on each side.

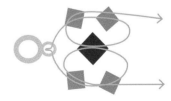

Continued over page...

Block Flower Bracelet

Step 6
Pick up one MC bead and pass both needles through this bead from opposite directions.

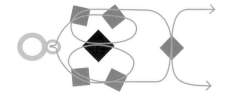

Step 7
Pick up one C2 bead on each needle.

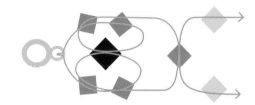

Step 8
Repeat Step 6.

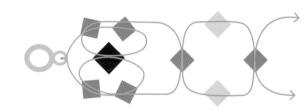

Step 9
Repeat Step 3 to Step 8 until you reach the required length. In step 7 of the last repeat, replace the bead with the other end of the clasp. Tie a series of knots around the clasp. Weave ends back through completed work to finish.

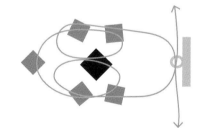

Tip
This technique can be applied to a bracelet or necklace.

Seaweed Bracelet

Seaweed Bracelet

Materials Needed
- Beading thread
- Size 11 or 12 beading needle
- 10g of each of 2 different coloured size 11 seed beads (SB)
- Feature beads of choice (if desired) (FB)
- Clasp of choice

Step 1
Cut a 1.5m length of thread, thread needle and attach one end of the clasp with a series of buttonhole stitches.

Step 2
Mix the two seed bead colours together and pick them up at random until you have the length required for the bracelet.

Step 3
Attach other end of clasp and pass needle back through the last two seed beads.

Step 4
Pick up 16 beads, miss the last bead and pass the needle through the next 5-6 beads.

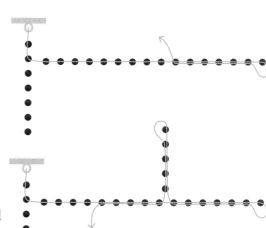

Step 5
Pick up 4-6 beads, miss the last bead and pass back through remaining beads on this branch and back up 5-6 more main beads on initial branch.

Step 6

Make another branch of 4-6 beads as per Step 5, then pass up to base row and through the next two beads on the base row.

Step 7

Repeat rows 4-6 until you reach the other end of the bracelet. Pass the thread back through the clasp and then back through three beads on the base row if you are going to add the embellishments such as the shells.

Step 8

String on 6 seed beads, a feature bead and a seed bead. Miss the last seed bead and pass back through all the beads back to the base row and then through four more beads on the base row.

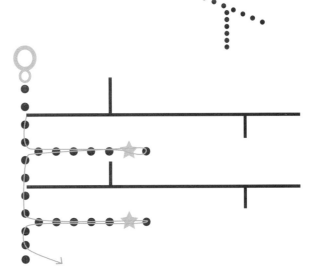

Step 9

Repeat this until you reach the end of the bracelet and end the thread by passing it through some of the fringing.

Bicone Triangle Bracelet

Materials Needed
- 1 packet of Delica beads in contrasting colour
- Size 10-12 beading needle
- Clasp of choice
- 90 - 100 of 4mm bicones
- Nymo beading thread

Step 1
Thread up approximately 2m of Nymo.

Step 2
Start by stringing 12 Delicas and slide them along to the end of the thread leaving abut a 10cm tail. Go back through all the beads and pull tight to form a circle. Tie a couple of knots. Go back through down the first 4 beads. Pull tight to form a loop.

Step 3
Put on 11 Delica beads and go back into the Delica bead that your thread is coming through in the original loop. Each loop will have a 'shared' Delica bead. After going through the 'shared' Delica bead go through 6 more beads in the second circle.

Step 4
Put on 11 Delicas and go back through the 'shared bead' of the previous loop (the one the thread is coming out of) and then through 6 beads on the new circle. Repeat this step for about 30 loops, or 5 bead loops longer than you need the bracelet length to be. The next steps will shorten the bracelet by about this amount. This is your chain of loops.

Step 5
After the last loop, come out of the 'shared' bead as usual.

Continued over page...

Step 6

String on 7 beads, one side of the clasp, three beads. Take the needle back through the 4th bead of the 7 beads, heading away from the clasp. Add 3 more beads and go into the 'shared' Delica from the opposite side that the thread is coming out of. Go through all the beads at least once more (three times in total is the most that the Delicas can handle comfortably. You should be back at your starting point before attaching the clasp. Now go through 3 Delicas in the first loop and you will be in the middle of the side of the chain loop.

Step 7

On each side of the loops there will be 5 Delicas. You will work through the 3rd (middle) Delica of each loop. Add a 4mm bicone and bring the thread through the 3rd Delica of each loop. Repeat to the end of the bracelet. Pull thread up tight, so that there is no thread showing between the bicones and the Delicas. This will align the Delica loops making them into a diamond-sided chain.

Step 8

When you get to the end of the bracelet, remove the stopper bead. Attach the other end of the clasp in the same way you did the other side (see Step 6). Once you are back at the 'shared' Delica bead again, go through 3 more Delicas on the other side of the chain loop.

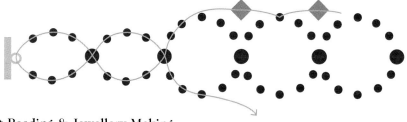

Step 9

Continue putting on the 4mm bicones and going through the 3rd Delica of each loop until you reach the other side again.

Step 10

You should be at the shared Delica bead again (of the first loop after the clasp). Now add the centre row of bicones.

Step 11

Add one 4mm bicone and go through the 'shared' Delica between the loops, so your thread follows a 'Z shape' when going back through next Delica. The bicone will sit slightly on top of the loop chain. Continue to add one 4mm bicone in this manner to the other end of the bracelet.

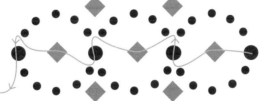

Step 12

Now go back through the 4mm bicones in the centre row to reinforce these. This time you will flip the bracelet upside down and work from the opposite side to make sure the crystals sit exactly in the middle of each loop.

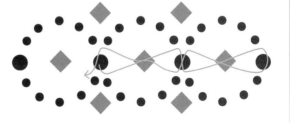

Step 13

When you have completed this tie off your thread and work in the tails from both the beginning and the end.

Bugle Bracelet

Materials Needed
- Beading thread
- 29 of 4mm fire polish beads (C4)
- 5g of size 11 seed beads (SB)
- Size 11 or 12 beading needle
- Approx. 72 of bugle beads (BB)
- Clasp of choice

Step 1
Cut a long length of thread and thread a needle. This is a bugle bead design so you do not want to cut the thread. Pick out the bugles that are the same size and have no jagged edges.

Step 2
Add 2BB and pass them down the thread leaving approximately 10cm of tail.

Step 3
Pass the needle back through the 1st BB and back through the 2nd BB.

Step 4
Add 1BB and pass the needle through the 2nd BB.

Step 5
Pass the needle back through the 3rd BB. Continue in this manner until you have 6 bugle beads.

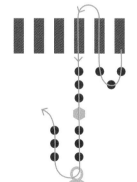

Step 6
Add 3SB, pass the needle through the 2nd BB. Pass the needle through the 3rd BB. Add 3SB, 1C4, 3SB, clasp and 3SB.

Continued over page...

Step 7
Pass the needle back through the 3SB, clasp, 3SB as in the diagram. Pass the needle through the C4. This will help reinforce the clasp.

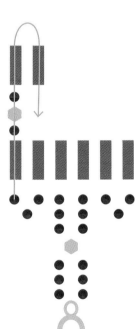

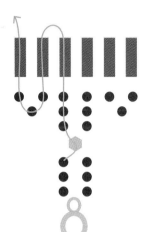

Step 8
Add 3SB, pass the needle up through the 4th BB and back down the 5th BB. Add 3SB and pass the needle through the 6th BB.

Step 9
Add 1SB, 1C4, 1SB, 2BB.

Step 10
Pass the needle back through the 1st BB, and back through the 2nd BB. Continue adding the bugles until you have 6.

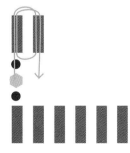

Start Beading & Jewellery Making

Step 11
Add 1SB, 1C4, 1SB and pass the needle though the BB as in the diagram.

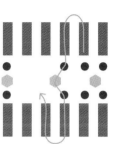

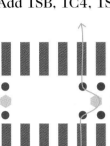

Step 12
Pass the needle through the 2nd BB. Add 1SB, pass the needle through the C4. Add 1SB and pass the needle through the 2nd BB below.

Step 13
Pass the needle through the 3rd BB. Add 1SB, 1C4, 1SB and pass the needle through the 3rd Bb above, then down through the 4th BB.

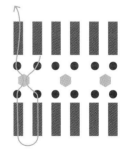

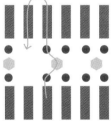

Step 14
Add 1SB, pass the needle through the C4. Add 1SB and pass the needle through the 4th BB below. Pass the needle up through the 5th BB.

Step 15
Add 1 SB, pass the needle though the C4. Add 1SB, pass the needle up through the 5th BB, and down through the 6th BB, and the next 4 beads coming out of the 6th BB as in the diagram.

Step 16
Repeat Step 9 to 15 until you have reached the required length. Attach the other end of the clasp as per Steps 6 - 8. Work the tail through the BB and cut off.

Bugle Bracelet

Spiral Rope Necklace

Materials Needed

- Fine or extra fine beading thread
- 20g of size 11 seed beads main colour (MC)
- 10g of size 11 seed beads contrast colour (CC)
- Size 11 or 12 beading needle
- Clasp of choice

Step 1

Cut a length of thread and thread a needle. Attach clasp of choice.

Step 2

String on 4CC and 3 MC and go back through the 4CC beads.

Step 3

Pick up 1CC and 3MC. Push the beads down the thread so that they sit against the work.

Step 4

Go back through 4CC beads (3 plus the one that you have just picked up), making sure as you pull the work up (not too tightly) the new outer beads fall to the left of the previous three. The work will spiral to the left and up.

Step 5

Pick up 1CC and 1MC, letting them fall down to the work, then go back through the last 4 CC beads.

Step 6

Repeat Step 5 for the desired length. Attach the other end of the clasp.

Tip

This technique can be applied to a necklace or bracelet.

Daisy Necklace or Bracelet

Materials Needed
- Beading thread
- Approx. 160 of 4mm fire polish beads (C4)
- 5g of size 11 seed beads (SB)
- Size 11 or 12 beading needle
- Approx. 80 of 6mm fire polish beads (C6)
- Clasp of choice

Step 1
Cut a length of thread and thread a needle. Thread on 3SB, 1C4, 1SB, 1C4, 1SB, 1C6, 1SB, 1C4, *1SB, 1C6, 1SB, 1C4. Repeat from * until you have the desired length ending with a 1C4. Push beads down leaving approximately 20cm of tail.

Step 2
Add 3SB, 1 clasp, 3SB, and pass back through to the 1st C6, as in the diagram.

Step 3
Add 1SB, pass the needle through the next C4.

Step 4
Add 1SB and pass the needle through the next C6.

Step 5
Repeat Step 3 - 4 until you have completed the row, coming out of the last C6. Pass the needle through the next 4 beads.

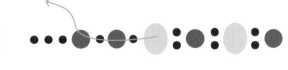

Step 6
Add 3SB, 1 clasp, pass the needle through the 3SB on the other side. Leave the tail for now as this will be finished later. If your work gets loose, pull on the tail to tighten it up.

Continued over page...

Daisy Necklace or Bracelet

Step 7

Pass the needle though the next 6 beads, coming out of the SB.

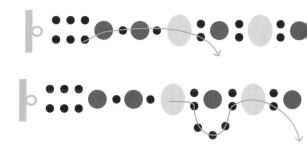

Step 8

Add 3SB, pass the needle through the next 3 beads, as in the diagram. Repeat Step 9 until you have completed the row, coming out of the last C6.

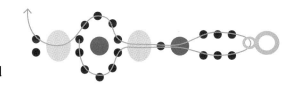

Step 9

Pass the needle through the beads to the other side of the last 3SB added. Repeat Step 9 on the other side of the work until you have completed the row, coming out the last C6.

Step 10

Pass needle through beads until it is coming through the last bead of the 1st 3SB loop.

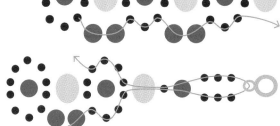

Step 11

Add 2C4, and pass the needle through the next 3SB of the previous row. Repeat until you reach the end, 1 bead before the last C6.

Step 12

Pass the needle through the beads, through the clasp, and back through the first 3SB loop on the other side. Repeat Step 12 until you have completed the row.

Step 13 - Finishing off. Work the needle down through the beads, as in the diagram and cut off. Finish off the tail end now as in diagram.

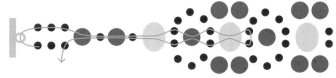

Hearts Necklace & Earrings

Hearts Necklace & Earrings

Materials Needed
- Tiger tail wire
- Crimp beads as required
- Pliers - flat nose or crimping, cutting
- Clasp of choice
- 2 eye pins per pair of earrings
- Shepherd's hook
- Heart shaped, or feature beads as required

Necklace

Step 1
Cut a length of tiger tail wire using cutting pliers. Do not use scissors. Tiger tail is a multi-stranded wire and will ruin scissors. Always use a good pair of pliers so that the cutting edge will last.

Step 2
Pass the tiger tail wire through a crimp, one end of the clasp, and then back through the crimp. Make the loop at the clasp end as small as possible but not too tight. Close off the crimps using the crimping or flat nose pliers.

Step 3
Thread the beads on in the sequence which you have decided until you reach the required length.

Step 4
Thread a crimp on the other end of the clasp, and then pass the wire back through the crimp bead. Close off the crimp as before.

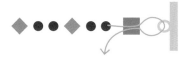

Step 5
Pass the end of the wire back through the bead and cut off.

Step 6
If you wish you can attach a charm to either or both of the loops.

Earrings
Step 1
On the eye pin, put on the sequence of beads that you have selected for the earrings.

Step 2
Bend the eye pin at a 90 degree angle to the beads and cut off any excess wire (leave approximately 1cm of wire after the beads).

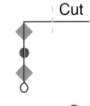

Step 3
Using the round nose pliers, roll back the eye pin to form a loop, whilst holding the beads firmly. When you are half of the way through the loop attach the Shepherd's hook and close off the loop.

Step 4
Repeat Steps 1 - 3 for the other earring.

Tip
This technique can be applied to a necklace, earrings or bracelet.

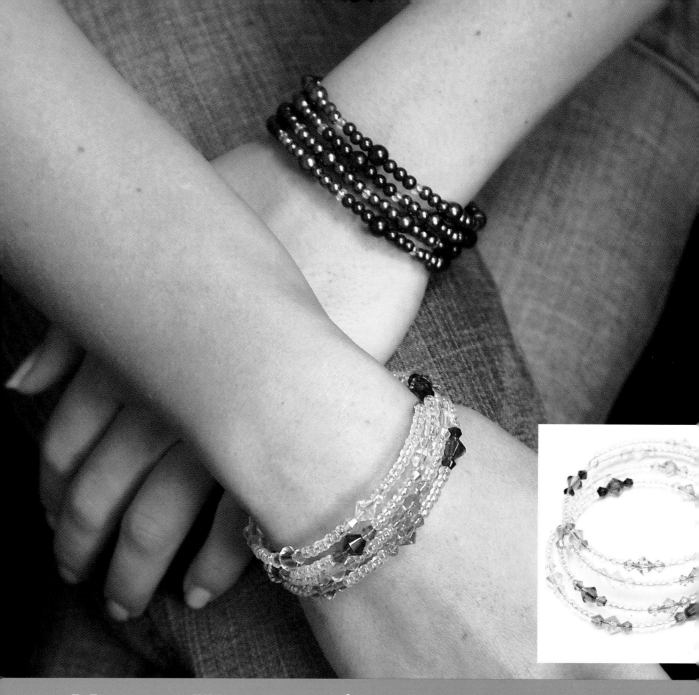

Memory Wire Bracelet

Materials Needed
- Bracelet size memory wire
- Round nose pliers
- Assorted beads (a mixture of small and large)

Step 1
Twist one end of the memory wire with the round nose pliers to form a loop.

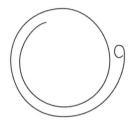

Step 2
Put beads on wire in any sequence, making sure to mix large and small and colours to make it interesting, until you have about 1cm length left on the wire.

Step 3
Holding the beads tight against each other, twist the other end of the wire with the round nose pliers to form a loop.

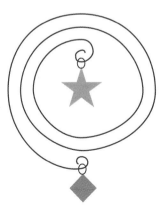

Step 4
If you wish you can attach a charm to either or both of the loops.

Spiral Necklace with Pearls

Materials Needed

- Beading thread
- 20g of size 11 seed beads (MC)
- 5g of size 11 seed beads (C3)
- Clasp of choice
- Size 11 or 12 beading needle
- 5g of size 11 seed beads (C2)
- 5g of 2.5mm Pearl beads (P)

Step 1

Cut a length of thread and thread a needle.

Step 2

Thread on 1P, 1C1, 1C2, 1MC bead, and thread needle back through all these beads, leaving a 20cm tail. Tie a knot and pass through the P. As this is a spiral it is important to make sure that the thread is always working in the same direction.

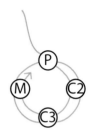

Step 3

Pick up 1P and pass through the C2 bead of previous row.

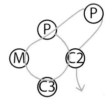

Step 4

Pick up a C2 bead and pass through the C3 bead of previous row.

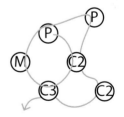

Continued over page...

Spiral Necklace with Pearls

Step 5
Pick up 1C3 and 2MC and pass through the P of the previous row (Step 3).

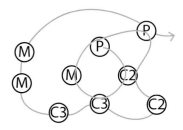

Step 6
Repeat Steps 3 - 5 increasing 1MC bead in each row until you reach the number required. The sample has 7MC in each row but you can increase to any number up to 12 beads.

Step 7
The repeat sequence will be: Pick up 1P and pass through the C2 bead of previous row. Pick up a C2 bead and pass through the C3 bead of previous row. Pick up 1C3 and 7MC and pass through the P of the previous row.

Step 8
An easy way to remember which bead is next is that you are picking up whatever bead your thread is coming through. For example, if your thread is in a P, you pick up a P, thread through C2, and then pick up C2.

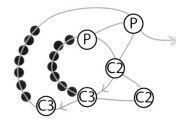

Step 9
Repeat Step 7 until you reach the required length.

Step 10
Repeat Step 6 in reverse, decreasing 1MC bead in each repeat until you have only 1MC bead.

Step 11
Attach clasp to each end of spiral.

● **Standard bead used in project**

● **Same type of bead but in a different colour**

● **Stop bead - Loop thread around a different bead twice about 20cm from the end to secure.**

Example:

Needle

Clasp

End clasp

Bicone bead

Any bead of same colour but larger = joining bead

Bugle bead

Crimp

Eye pin

Clam

The Get Creative series of books are a collaborative effort of many creative and talented people. The publisher wishes to thank all of them for their hard work and dedication to the series, in an effort to retain the essential role that crafts and D.I.Y. plays in all our lives.

First Published in 2004 by Get Creative Pty Ltd
Locked Bag 4321, South Melbourne, Australia 3205
www.getcreative.com.au   info@getcreative.com.au
Toll Free Hotline 1300 662 742 (In Australia)

Created by Jono Gelfand
Produced by Brooke Hannaford
Creative Director Veronica Cunningham
Graphic Design by Stela Cuevas & Sonia Barras
Photography by Mick Guerin
Projects Designed & Made by Mary Farrugia
Acknowledgements: Jacquie Byron & Nicole Croswell

Copyright – all rights reserved. No part of this book may be reproduced by any means without prior permission in writing.

National Library of Australia Cataloguing-in-Publication data:
Get creative : start beading & jewellery making.

Includes index.
 ISBN 1 920954 22 8.

1. Jewelery making. 2. Beadwork. 3. Beads. I. Title.

739.27

Disclaimer:
Get Creative makes available to you these patterns, designs, and written instructions. We expressly grant you the right to copy the patterns, designs, and written instructions, and to construct the projects for your personal use.

All care has been taken to ensure that the information contained in this book and that the activities suggested have been presented in a responsible manner and are not dangerous or harmful, but no responsibility is accepted for any errors or omissions. We cannot, however, be responsible for human error, typographical mistakes, or variations in individual work.

Information and instructions given in this book are presented in good faith, but no warranty is given nor results guaranteed. Please always take the time to read all manufacturer's instructions and warnings before using any product. Please keep all harmful or dangerous products out of reach of children at all times.

get creative